Learn About Books

Space Travel

TEXT BY STEPHEN ATTMORE

ILLUSTRATED BY TONY GIBBONS

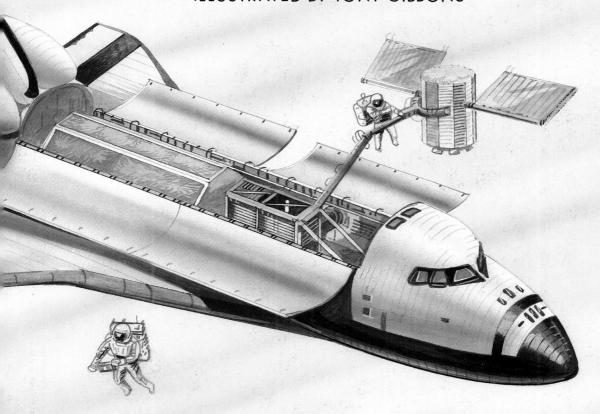

BRIMAX BOOKS • NEWMARKET • ENGLAND

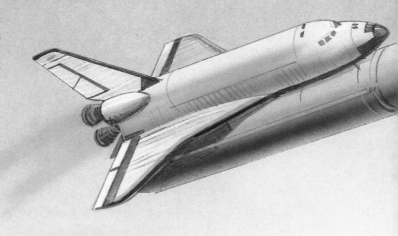

10
9
8
7
6
5
4
3
2
1 . . .

We have lift-off! Here is the American space shuttle. It has three engines and two extra rockets. They all fire together. Look for the big fuel tank. The shuttle is taking people up into space.

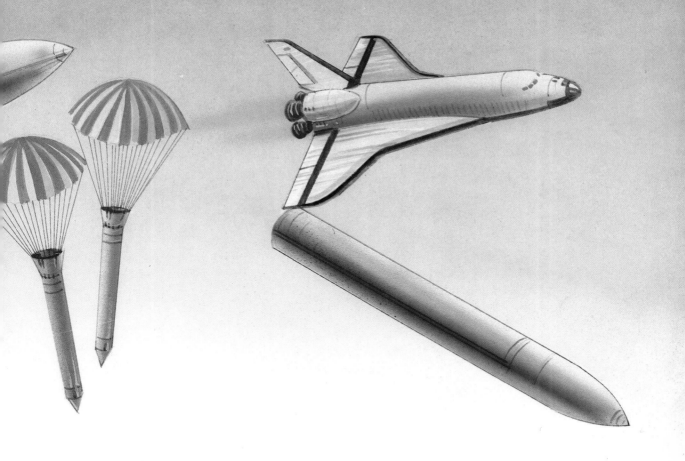

About two minutes after lift-off
the shuttle lets the booster
rockets go. They fall down to
Earth. Six minutes later the fuel
tank is dropped. It is empty now.
When it is in space the shuttle
orbits the Earth. It goes round
and round us.

People sent into space by the
Russians are called cosmonauts.
People sent into space by the
Americans are called astronauts.
Look at these astronauts training.
They are in a huge water tank.

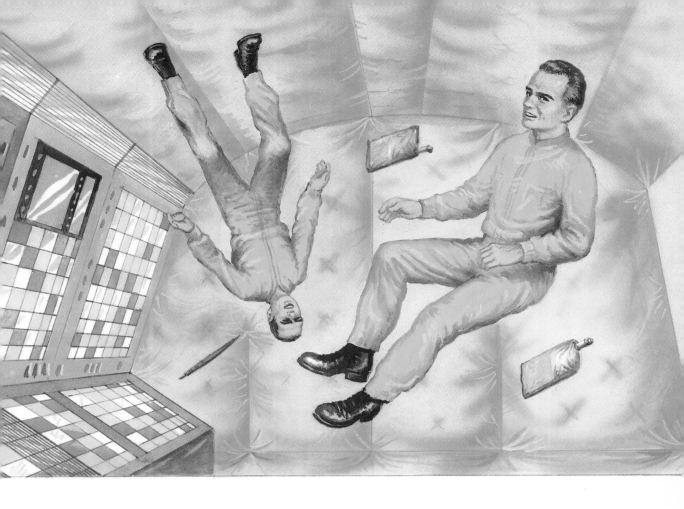

What happens when you throw a ball
in the air? It comes down again.
A force called gravity pulls it
down to Earth. People in space
find that there is no gravity.
Look at the people floating in
their spacecraft. If they let go
of something it floats away.

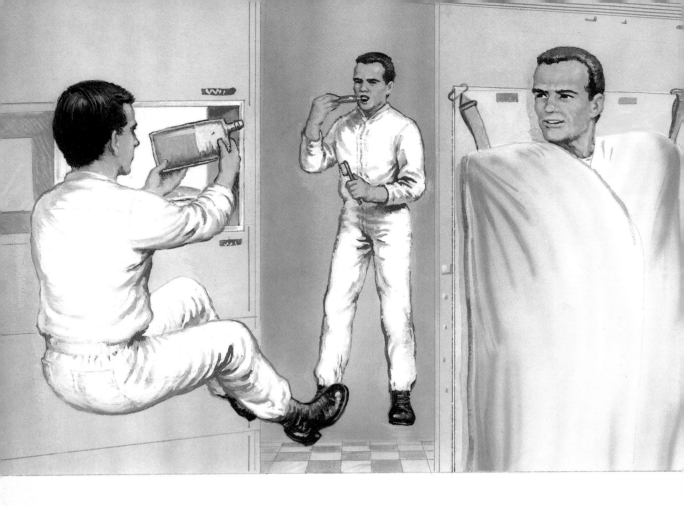

Life in space has its problems!
Food is kept in special packs.
You cannot pour drinks into
glasses. You squirt the drink into
your mouth. People in space cannot
sleep in beds – they and the bed-
clothes would float away. Look at
the astronaut in a sleeping bag.

Look at this astronaut. He is space walking. The long tube leads from the craft to his spacesuit. He breathes air through it.

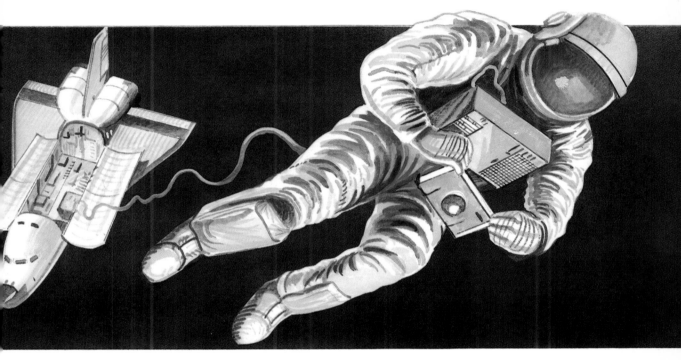

Can you see the special pack worn by this astronaut? He can move away from the craft.

A dog called Laika was the first space traveller. She was sent into orbit by the Russians in 1957. Laika stayed in space for seven days.

The first person to go into space was a Russian. In 1961 Yuri Gagarin circled the Earth in a spacecraft called Vostok 1.

John Glenn was the first American to go into space. He circled the Earth in 1962.

A year later the Russians sent the first woman into space. Valentina Tereshkova went round the Earth 48 times.

On 20 July 1969 an American
spacecraft landed on the Moon.
Astronaut Neil Armstrong climbed
down a ladder. He was the first
person to step on to the Moon.
He was followed by Edwin Aldrin.

Look at this astronaut driving
a strange car. It is a special car
for getting about on the Moon.
Can you see Earth in the sky?

Look at the cosmonauts inside the house in space. It is a space station. The cosmonauts live and work here. They do tests to find out about space. After a few weeks they return to Earth. Then other cosmonauts go to the space station.

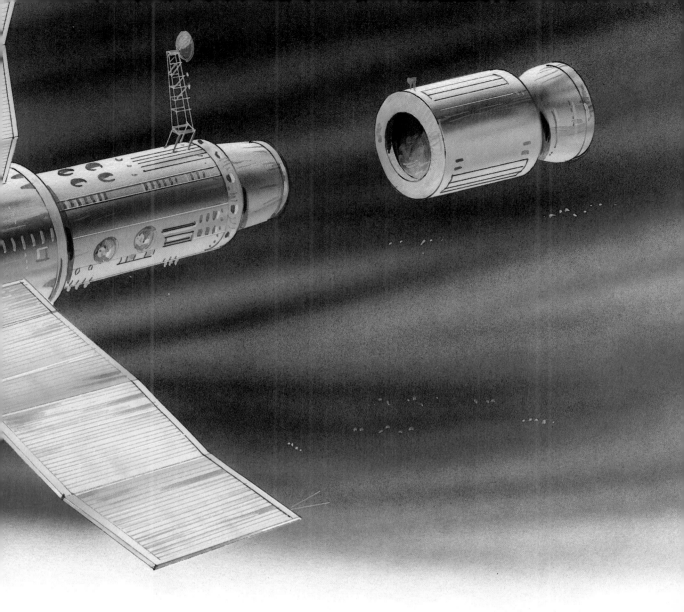

Can you see the small spacecraft
about to dock? It is going to join
up with the space station. There
are no people on board the small
craft. It is bringing food, water
and fuel. It has come from Earth.

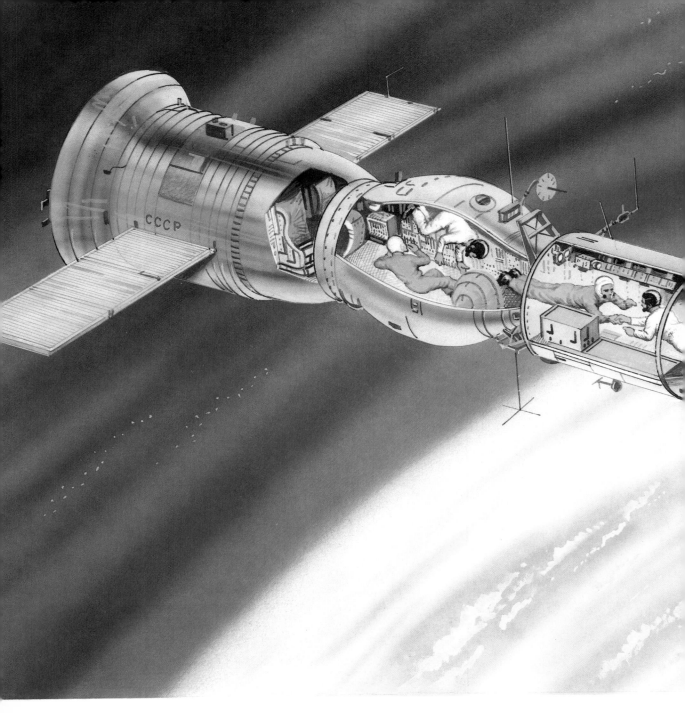

In July 1975 astronauts met cosmonauts in space for the first time. American and Russian spacecrafts joined together.

Parts of the two crafts are not shown. Look for the Americans and the Russians shaking hands. Which ones are the cosmonauts?

These astronauts have splashed down in the sea. They are back to Earth. The big balloons on the American spacecraft help it to float. A rescue boat is on its way to pick up the astronauts.

When the space shuttle returns to Earth it lands like a plane. It uses its wings to fly. The space shuttle lands on a runway.

Russian space-craft come down on land. As they get near to Earth, the cosmonauts eject. They are thrown out of the spacecraft.

What will space stations be like
in the future? This one looks like
a city in space. A space shuttle
is carrying people from Earth to
the space station. It will take
other people back on its return.

Will people live on the Moon?
Many years from now, people may
live in a Moon city like this.
Think about it. You may be able
to take a holiday on the Moon!

In this book you have read about people in space. What are these people doing?

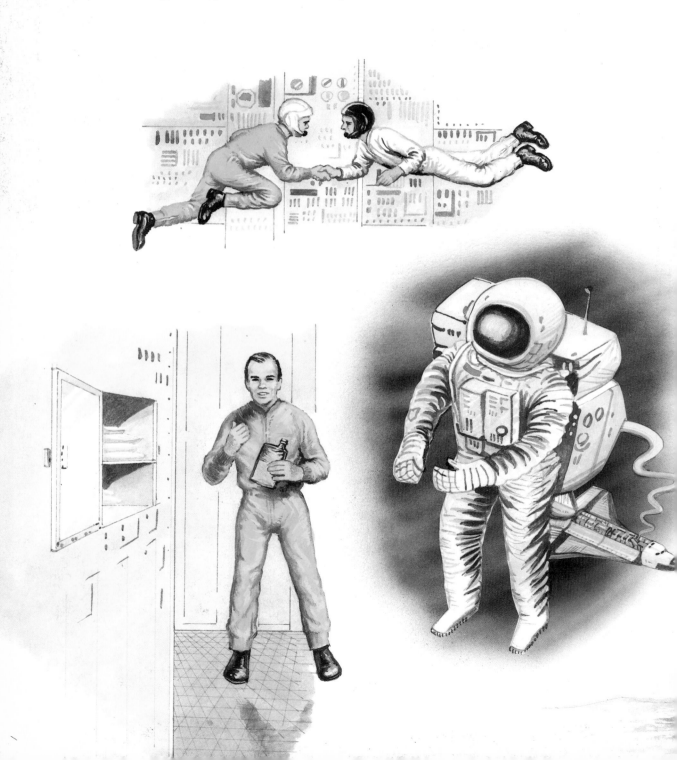